CRITICAL WORLD ISSUES

The Arms Trade

Critical World Issues

Abortion	**Food Technology**
Animal Rights	**Genetic Engineering**
The Arms Trade	**Genocide**
Capital Punishment	**Human Rights**
Consumerism	**Poverty**
Drugs	**Racism**
Equal Opportunities	**Refugees**
Euthanasia	**Terrorism**

CRITICAL WORLD ISSUES

The Arms Trade

Dan Marcovitz

MASON CREST
PHILADELPHIA

Understanding the Arms Trade

Taken from his home at a young age, Kendu Mbosi has seen the damage that the *arms trade* has caused in just one country. In his time as a child soldier, he has come across a wide range of weapons designed and made in many countries around the world. These have caused devastation to his comrades, friends, home, and family.

Kendu's Story

"My name is Kendu Mbosi. When I was a teenager, I was taken from my home in northern Uganda by an armed rebel group fighting the Ugandan government. I was taught how to fire guns and *mortars*, and when I showed fear or refused to do what they said, I was beaten.

A young African man holds an Russian-made AK-47 assault rifle. Such weapons are relatively easy to buy in the developing world—in some places, an AK-47 can be bought for as little as $15, or even for a bag of grain. They are also easy to use: with minimal training, even a child can wield one of these deadly weapons.

Within a few weeks, I was part of the rebel force. There were other children of my age, and several were even younger. Many of the weapons the force owned were far older than we were. Some guns and mortars were from the United States, others were French. While I was there, the rebels received two rocket launchers which were from Eastern Europe and looked new. No one would say how they had gotten them.

Fighting was terrifying, and I saw many people die. I was lucky and managed to escape and be reunited with my family. The village we used to live in is no longer there—much of it was destroyed by bombs.

We all now live in a large town in southern Uganda. Life is hard: We miss our village, and I have to help care for my younger sister. She lost her left leg when her bicycle rode over

 Words to Understand in This Chapter

arms trade—the buying and selling of weapons and defense equipment used in conflict.

casualty—a person who is hurt or killed during an accident, war, etc.

Cold War—the nonviolent conflict between the US and the former Soviet Union after 1945.

embargo—a government order that limits trade in some way.

mortar—a short light cannon used to shoot shells high into the air.

reconnaissance—military activity in which soldiers, airplanes, etc., are sent to find out information about an enemy.

Soviet Union—Union of Soviet Socialist Republics (USSR): a country from 1922–1991 that included 15 republics in Eastern Europe and Northern Asia, the largest of which was Russia.

A cargo of weapons and ammunition intended for a rebel group in Africa.

a landmine buried near our village. I try to forget the bad memories of the fighting, but sometimes they return. I know that there would be troubles between different groups in Uganda even if there were no weapons, but I think the weapons make it much harder, especially on ordinary people. I was lucky. My mother, my sister, and I are still alive."

Beginnings of the Arms Trade

The arms industry is engaged in researching, designing, and building military technology, particularly weapons and protection against weapons, such as armor. The arms trade is the buying and selling of weapons and defense equipment. It is a vast industry, one of the largest in the world, and it has major effects on how millions of people live their lives.

The arms trade is not a new or even a 20th-century phenomenon. It can be traced back hundreds of years to the invention of new weapons and their demand by different groups, forces, and countries. The arrival of gunpowder in Europe from the late 14th century onward led to a demand by various armies for gunpowder-charged muskets and cannons.

During the 18th and 19th centuries, the Industrial Revolution and the rise of large factories saw companies able to build large numbers of more complicated weapons, such as machine guns and massive warships. These arms were touted for sale by powerful weapons traders, such as Sir Basil Zaharoff, "the merchant of death," who dealt arms in 19th century Europe and Russia and became one of the richest people in the world. These businessmen did not care who bought their weapons, selling arms to all sides engaged in a conflict.

The two world wars of the 20th century saw massive jumps in weapons technology, the range of weapons available, and the numbers built and sold. For example, at the start of World War I (1914-1918), aircraft were flimsy, unreliable machines. They were used in very small numbers and in a limited role as *reconnaissance* aircraft, or "spotters," reporting the positions of troops and guns on the ground. By the end of the war, however, the combatants had developed a range of different types of aircraft, including bombers and fighters that were able to fly higher, farther, and faster than any aircraft that had existed at the start of the conflict.

The first tanks were also introduced in World War I, and although these machines were slow and cumbersome at first, they went on to change the tactics and structure of modern warfare. Both tanks and aircraft advanced quickly and were built in huge numbers in the period between the two wars, eventually equipping the forces that fought in World War II

B-25 bombers are assembled at the North American Aviation facility in Kansas City, 1942.

Today, weapons are for sale openly in the central market of Kabul, Afghanistan. The huge numbers of small arms readily available in Africa, Asia, and Central America are a legacy of the Cold War, when the United States and Soviet Union supplied weapons to governments or rebel groups willing to fight for their strategic interests.

(1939-1945). Enormous arms companies, such as Boeing and Lockheed in the US, were established and grew to supply these new, sophisticated weapons in ever-increasing numbers.

The Cold War

From the end of World War II until the early 1990s, many countries of the world aligned themselves with one of the two superpowers, the United States or the *Soviet Union*. The world's two most powerful nations were hostile to and suspicious of each other but never directly fought. This period is known as the *Cold War*. It saw an expansion of the arms industry and the development of giant weapons and aerospace companies. In the late 1970s and early 1980s, more arms were bought and sold than at any other time in history.

The two superpowers built up larger and larger stockpiles of weapons within their own borders while spending vast sums on research into new types of arms, including nuclear weapons. In addition, the US, Soviet Union, and their major allies supplied many other nations and forces with large amounts of military equipment. Sometimes, these arms were donated or offered at greatly-reduced prices to governments in order to build alliances against the other superpower. Some of these weapons supplies were donated to rebel groups in countries whose governments were friendly to the other superpower. The goal was to topple these governments and replace them with others that would become allies.

Arms since the Cold War

With the collapse of the Soviet Union at the start of the 1990s, there were no longer two rival superpowers. The threat of all-out war between the world's most powerful nations receded, and the US, Russia, and many of their major allies scaled down the size of their military forces. This resulted in a large surplus of arms, many of which were sold to other countries at greatly-reduced prices. New military spending decreased a great deal but not at a rate that many peace campaigners had hoped for. Today's remaining superpower, the US, still spends an enor-

The Arms
that Are Traded

Arms manufacturers sell a huge, bewildering array of items, from the simplest policeman's nightstick and the smallest bullet to complex electronic navigation systems and the largest aircraft carrier.

A typical major arms fair will have dozens of stands selling thousands of different products. Most of the arms on sale are conventional weapons—those arms which are not chemical, biological, or nuclear weapons. Major conventional weapons include aircraft; submarines; warships such as destroyers and aircraft carriers; tanks and armored vehicles; and large artillery guns and missile systems.

These weapons form the most expensive and profitable side of the arms trade, accounting for as much as 80 percent of the value of all arms sales. New conventional weapons tend to be

A variety of weapons and equipment on display at a trade show in Milan, Italy. Countries and organizations wishing to buy weapons can view them and deal with suppliers at arms fairs that are held all over the world.

incredibly expensive. A Lockheed Martin F-22 Raptor jet fighter, for example, costs $150 million and can carry a range of missiles, many of which cost several hundred thousand dollars each. One of its missiles, the AIM120 AMRAAM, costs $1.78 million per unit.

Wide Range of Arms Sales

Police forces, prisons, and other security organizations in many countries around the world buy arms, such as handguns and assault rifles, as well as a range of products designed to restrain prisoners and control crowds. These include armored vehicles, water cannons, gas sprays, riot shields, and electroshock devices, such as Taser stun guns. Many of these items have caused concern among human rights groups since they have been used for torture and beatings.

Although weaponry is an important part of many arms sales, vast sums are also spent on materials and services that are related to these weapons, such as maintenance and training

 Words to Understand in This Chapter

civilian—a person who is not a member of the military or of a police or firefighting force.

small arms—weapons that are fired while being held in one hand or both hands. These include handguns, rifles, shotguns, and assault rifles.

subsidence—the gradual sinking of land.

weapons of mass destruction—weapons that can destroy entire cities, or can kill large numbers of people.

This submachine gun was manufactured by Heckler and Koch. The company has also brokered legal arms deals with armed forces all around the world.

contracts, as well as transportation equipment. For example, the US Air Force spends $2.6 million to train a fighter pilot and $600,000 to train an airlift pilot. Flight simulators that cost $10,000 each are used to reduce training costs of pilots' flight time in aircraft. As military weapons have become more and more complex, services such as training have become an important commodity. They are promoted and sold at arms fairs and meetings almost as much as bullets, bombs, and other weapons.

Although handguns make up only 34 percent of the more than 310 million firearms owned in the United States, approximately 80 percent of gun-related homicides are committed with a handgun.

The Small Arms Trade

Small arms are usually defined as weapons for personal use: handguns, rifles, light machine guns, and weapons that can be operated by a single person, such as grenades, mortars, and antipersonnel landmines.

The building and selling of large, conventional weapons such as jet aircraft is concentrated in a handful of wealthier countries, but small arms are manufactured legally in more than 1,000 factories in over 100 countries throughout the world. Out of these countries, many developing countries are producing and selling small arms abroad. The legal trade in small arms was estimated in 2011 to be worth between $8.5 billion worldwide. The illegal trade in small arms, which are easy to hide and transport, is feared to be even larger.

It is estimated that over 875 million small arms are in circulation around the world—one for every eight people. During the Cold War, many nations were flooded with small arms by powerful nations such as the US and former Soviet Union. The arms remain in these countries, while stockpiles of old weapons from previous conflicts are traded and used in other conflicts. Many small arms are easy to maintain and last for decades, such as the Russian-designed AK-47 assault rifle. These weapons are often cheap enough to sustain high demand, including from criminals and rebel militia groups.

Weapons of Mass Destruction

Weapons of mass destruction (WMDs) are weapons designed to kill large numbers of people. WMDs include nuclear weapons, chemical weapons, and biological weapons.

An member of the Suri tribe of Ethiopia aims an AK-47 assault rifle. The AK-47 is easy to use and maintain. Because of this, it remain a popular choice of weapon for many rebel or irregular forces.

Biological or germ warfare involves using parts or products of living organisms to cause harm. By trying to poison the drinking wells of a castle or throwing the bodies of plague victims into an opposing army, armed forces have used biological warfare tactics since medieval times.

The first major use of chemical warfare was during World War I, when chlorine gas, mustard gas, and phosgene gas were first deployed by German forces against the Allies. Although there have been hundreds of nuclear weapons tests, only two have ever been used in war—the two atomic bombs dropped on the Japanese cities of Hiroshima and Nagasaki by the US in 1945 towards the end of World War II.

The military forces of almost all countries have studied the effects of WMDs and realize that they have limited military usefulness: their effects are hard to control, many contaminate areas for decades afterward, and their use on another country is likely to trigger an extreme response. International agreements, such as the Nuclear Nonproliferation Treaty of 1970 and the 1925 Geneva Protocol, have also sought to outlaw the

In many conflicts, rebel groups will mount heavy weapons such as machine guns in the back of pickup trucks. This creates a fighting vehicle that can move quickly and has more firepower than the small arms carried by most rebels.

A squadron of Russian Su-27 fighter jets flies over an airshow. The jets are relatively inexpensive at about $22 million each. (Some other advanced fighter jets, such as the F-35 pictured on page 35 of this book, cost well over $100 million.) Despite the amount it costs to run the Su-27 fighter, the aircraft serves in the air forces of many developing countries, including Angola, Eritrea, Ethiopia, Indonesia, Kazakhstan, Uzbekistan, and Vietnam.

spread and use of WMDs.

However, fears remain about these devastating weapons. Chemical weapons, for example, were used in the 1980s during both the Iran-Iraq war and by Iraqi forces on the Kurdish *civilian* population. During the Syrian Civil War in 2013, the Syrian military was reported to use sarin nerve gas on civilians in the Ghouta area of Damascus, killing 734. The total death toll due to chemical weapons during the Syrian Civil War was over 1,400—including 400 children. This prompted military threats by the international community, led by the US and Russia jointly, which resulted in the Syrian government agreeing to give up its chemical weapons.

Nations with WMDs

At least 26 nations are known to have had programs producing nuclear, chemical, or biological weapons. There are nine nations with declared nuclear weapons: the United States, UK, Russia, China, France, India, Israel, North Korea, and Pakistan.

A United Nations inspector from the Netherlands measures the volume of a chemical weapon in a container in Iraq, 1991.

A member of a demining team uses a bomb sniffing dog to find unexploded landmines in Bunia, Democratic Republic of the Congo.

Iran potentially has nuclear capabilities. No countries are known to have biological weapons, but eight may have them. Four countries—the US, Russia, Syria, and North Korea—have chemical weapons, and 16 others may have them.

A key concern is that the technology required to make these weapons could fall into the hands of terrorist groups that might actually use them. Many of the substances or equipment needed to make WMDs are easily available or are dual-use products, meaning that they have a peacetime use as well as a military one, such as nuclear technology that can be used to power cities or destroy them.

The Danger of Landmines

Antipersonnel landmines are hidden killers. Buried just below the land's surface, they are hard to detect and explode when pressure is placed on them from above, whether the victim is a soldier or civilian, adult or child. Landmines are one of the few weapons to remain dangerous long after a war or conflict in

 The Cost of Landmines

Some 54 countries have produced more than 340 models of antipersonnel landmines. They cost as between $3 and $75 to produce and are relatively easy to deploy. By contrast, it costs between $300 and $1,000 to locate and destroy a single mine, which must be done by individual removal.

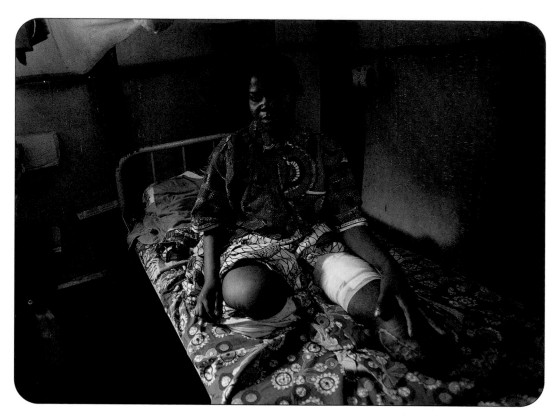

This African man lost both of his legs when he stepped on a hidden landmine.

which they were used has finished. Deaths attributed to forty-year-old landmines have been reported. Many minefields remain unknown, as they were created without warning signs, and barriers to outline their perimeters have since disappeared. In addition, some mines have been moved to new areas by floods or *subsidence*. The impact of landmines around the world is huge. Poor farming communities have been particularly hard hit. Thousands of acres of land, often with fertile soil, have had to be abandoned because of landmines planted in the vicinity.

It is difficult to know how many landmines are buried throughout the world, but estimates are in the tens of millions. In 2014, 3,678 people were killed by landmines in 54 countries; the death toll represented a 12 percent increase from 2013. On average, 10 deaths are caused by a landmine every day. Eighty percent of landmine victims are civilians, with 39 percent being children. In the last decade, an estimated hundreds of thousands of survivors have been left with severe disabilities due to landmines, which cause horrific injuries and often loss of limbs.

New technologies—in the form of special radar systems and mine-clearing robots—are being deployed, but the majori-

A variety of landmines found in Northern Iraq.

These Indian soldiers are manning a checkpoint in the region of Jammu and Kashmir, an area whose territory is disputed by the nations of India and Pakistan.

ty of mine location and removal is done by hand. Mine-clearing personnel use a range of tools, including metal detectors and metal prodders, to probe the ground. Sometimes dogs are used to locate the scent of an explosive mine. Clearing a mined area, though, is a slow, expensive, and risky business. It takes approximately 100 times longer to clear an area of mines than to sow it with mines in the first place. In 2014, 200 km2 was cleared, destroying more than 230,000 antipersonnel mines and 11,500 antivehicle mines in the world.

 ## Text-Dependent Questions

1. Provide three reasons why countries are reluctant to use WMDs.
2. How serious of a problem are landmines? Give statistics to support your claim.

 ## Research Project

Using the Internet or your school library, research the topic of weapons of mass destruction, and answer the following question: "Should WMDs be banned in all countries?"

Some believe WMDs should be banned in all countries because they cause huge numbers of casualties and injuries, many of whom are civilians and children. War may be inevitable in the world, but WMDs make war much more destructive. It is hypocritical for some countries to have WMDs while condemning WMDs in other countries that are deemed "dangerous" or "oppressive." Others argue that WMDs should be allowed in some countries that have proven to protect the international community. If the UN approves, these countries can have the firepower to confront nations that might use WMDs to hurt civilians or invade other nations.

Write a two-page report, using data you have found in your research to support your conclusion, and present it to your class.

3

The People Involved in the Arms Trade

An arms sale, or or *transaction*, is usually shown publicly as a deal negotiated between two governments or between a government and a company. Behind the scenes, however, the buying and selling of arms can be far more complicated.

Most of the world's arms are bought by governments who are known as *state actors*. Nonstate actors who also buy arms, often illegally, are usually rebels or groups that seek to topple the government of a country. Among the state actors, the US government remains the single biggest customer for arms, nearly all of which are bought from companies based on its own soil. The biggest buyers of arms from other countries tend to be Asian and Middle Eastern nations: from 2010 to 2014, the top five arms importers were India, Saudi Arabia, China,

An Israeli police officer stands guard over the illicit weapons cargo found aboard a ship in the Israeli port of Ashdod in March 2011. The weapons, including C-704 anti-ship missiles, were destined for Palestinian militant organizations in the Gaza Strip.

4

Benefits
of the Arms Trade

T he arms trade makes up four percent of the entire world's trade—$76 billion of a total $19.06 trillion. Billions of dollars change hands between arms buyers and sellers. Such an enormous industry, one of the world's largest, could not continue if both buyers and sellers did not believe there were benefits. The debate is over whether these benefits are important enough to justify such great costs.

Every individual, group, and nation strives to feel secure and safe. Governments have a duty to protect their populations and the territories that they inhabit. For centuries, this has been a key reason for nations building strong military forces and equipping them with effective weapons.

As a symbol of the amount of money the US spends on weapons, the Pentagon, just outside Washington, D.C., serves as the headquarters of the world's most powerful military force.

Armed for Peace

Defense is the most frequently given reason for buying arms today and is backed by international laws and treaties that give nations the right to protect their borders. Some countries have developed valuable industries or have discovered extremely profitable deposits of raw materials, such as oil or diamonds. Many countries in this situation, including the oil-producing nations of the Middle East, fear that they may be invaded for their valuable resources. In 1990, Saddam Hussein's Iraq invaded Kuwait, one main reason being Kuwait's rich petroleum resources. These countries spend a large proportion of the wealth generated by these precious resources on arms to protect themselves.

Assistance for vulnerable countries or rising unrest can come from ally nations or the UN. UN Peacekeeping Forces consist of civilian police, observers, and armed soldiers volunteered by their governments. Peacekeepers have been employed around the world to restore or maintain peace, help disarm former fighters, and assist in rebuilding efforts. In 2015, there were 16 UN peacekeeping operations with 106,245 uniformed

 Words to Understand in This Chapter

deterrent—something that makes someone decide not to do something.

prestige purchasing—to buy goods or services to impress others.

strategic balance—distributing arms to countries in a region so as to achieve a desired level of equilibrium in military power and keep peace.

UN peacekeepers are noticeable for their bright blue helmets and the white vehicles they drive.

personnel, 16,791 civilian personnel, and 1,710 volunteers. The arms carried by peacekeepers are considered vital for them to perform their duties, and even with their defense equipment, there were 1,620 peacekeeper deaths in 2015.

Deterrence of Conflict

Arms may be bought but not actually used in the hope that a country's military strength will make another country decide against attacking or invading. This is known as a *deterrent*, and the most well-known example occurred during the Cold

A "Peacekeeper" missile blasts clear of its silo. During the Cold War, both the US and the Soviet Union stockpiled hundreds of intercontinental ballistic missiles (ICBMs), which are capable of hitting a target thousands of miles away. The Peacekeeper was America's most powerful, accurate and technologically advanced ICBM deterrent from 1986 to 2005.

War with nuclear weapons. The US and Soviet Union stock-piled vast numbers of nuclear warheads so that a massive attack by one nation would leave the other with enough capability to launch an equally huge attack on the other. Some argue that this example is proof of how arms can be a deterrent. Others point to how a buildup of non-nuclear arms has not acted as a deterrent in many of the conflicts currently occurring around the world.

Prestige Purchasing

The governments of many countries view their armed forces as an important symbol of their independence and power. The leaders of some nations buy large weapons, such as aircraft carriers or the latest jet fighters, in the belief that owning such weapons will make their country gain more respect from the world. They may also see a link between military might and political power, leading to spending huge sums of money to expand their armed forces. They may then openly display these forces in shows of strength meant to impress and intimidate their own people and other countries around the world. This is known as *prestige purchasing*.

Prestige purchasing is often extremely wasteful since the weapons bought may not be suited to the region in which they are to operate. An example of this is Thailand's proposed buying of two Israeli submarines despite the fact that much of the local waters around the country are very shallow, making submarines an easy target.

The sudden and cheap availability of some weapons can also lead to prestige purchasing. For example, the end of the

Many workers in richer countries are dependent on jobs in the defense industry.

Influence through the Arms Trade

Countries and companies that sell arms use a number of arguments to justify their sales besides money. One of the most important is that selling arms can increase a country's influence in a part of the world. Arms sales have been used to bring two nations closer together to form an alliance, as they did during the Cold War, when weapons were sold to countries allied to the US and the Soviet Union, respectively. Arms sales are also often part of a package of other useful deals for sharing information and resources or supplying nonmilitary goods and services.

Arms sales can be used to help control other countries, as buyers become reliant on supplies of arms and expertise from the selling country. Weapons are made up of hundreds or even thousands of delicate and complex parts. The possibility of losing access to spare parts or further sales can influence countries to remain friendly and provide benefits in return. Countries that sell arms develop high levels of knowledge about their customers' military strengths and weaknesses. Not only do they know the abilities of the weapons they sell to them, but they also learn much about a nation's total arsenal and the size of their forces. This can become vital information should both nations come to conflict—another reason for the arms-buying nation to continue as an ally.

The US Arms Trade in Numbers

Exports in general benefit a country's economy because they bring foreign money in and generate jobs, and the US gains these advantages as the world's largest arms exporter. SIPRI

5

Problems Caused by the Arms Trade

For some people, the arms trade is simply a business of selling products, and they feel that people involved in creating and selling weapons should not be held responsible for how they are used. However, many critics of the arms trade believe that selling large amounts of arms around the world helps to create conflicts, causes small-scale *skirmishes* to mushroom into larger-scale wars, and results in physical and economic misery for millions of people.

Without arms supplies, wars would still be possible, but many people believe they would be easier to contain, result in fewer casualties, end more quickly, and have greater potential to rebuild in peace afterward. The relatively ready availability of arms can also prompt peoples or governments to seek a vio-

Buildings destroyed by Israeli bombing in the city of Beirut, Lebanon, 2006. The easy availability of weapons has enabled those opposed to the state of Israel to launch regular rocket attacks over the border. Israel retaliates by bombing the places—often civilian areas—from which the rockets were launched, causing innocent casualties and property destruction.

lent solution to a problem when peaceful means may be viable. Arms are frequently used on a country's own people, who may not have taken up arms but simply disagreed with their government's policies. The use of weapons on peaceful demonstrators, critics, and protesters has—in countries from Indonesia and Sri Lanka to Uganda, Colombia, and Angola—caused troubles to escalate into violent conflict.

Most Common Uses of Arms

Most of the arms actually used today are not directly for defending a country's borders or resources from attack by another country. Instead, many nations have used their arms to invade other countries. Many more have used their weapons on their own people, either to suppress local opposition to their government or to fight bitter, long-running wars with rebel groups.

 Words to Understand in This Chapter

asylum—protection given by a government to someone who has left another country in order to escape being harmed.

infrastructure—the basic equipment and framework (such as roads and bridges) that are needed for a country, region, or organization to function properly.

intrastate—existing or occurring within a state or country.

persecution—the act of continually treating in a cruel and harmful way.

refugee—someone who has been forced to leave a country because of war or for religious or political reasons.

skirmish—a brief and usually unplanned fight during a war.

uninhabitable—a place that cannot be lived in.

Yemeni soldiers on duty at a checkpoint in the Hadramaut Valley. Since 2015 Yemen has been torn by civil war. Regional powers Iran and Saudi Arabia have supplied arms to opposing factions, hoping to gain influence over the region.

Data from the Peace Research Institute Oslo (PRIO) revealed that in 2006, there were 32 conflicts in the world, with 27 *intrastate*, or in-country, conflicts between a government and a non-government group. Five conflicts in 2006 were "internationalized intrastate," in-country conflicts between a government and a non-government group with either or both sides receiving military support from another country. None were "interstate," conflicts between two countries, though they do exist today.

Indian Army tanks participate in the annual Republic Day Parade in Delhi. India has the world's third-largest army, after China and the United States.

Arms Races

An arms race is a continuing cycle of rival nations feeling threatened by one another and buying or producing more and more weapons for military superiority. The Cold War saw a massive arms race between the two rival superpowers, the US and Soviet Union.

Today, arms races are occurring in several regions around the world, including between China and Taiwan as well as India and Pakistan. Internal arms races can also occur within a country when a rebel group's purchases of weapons prompts the national government to spend more on arms. These arms races can create extra tension and instability which can spill over into conflict. Even if an uneasy peace is kept, the money spent on weapons may escalate, depriving peaceful sectors of government spending, such as hospitals and schools as well as investment in industry and technology.

The Direct Human Cost

The Human Security Report Project documented 10,241,076 casualties from 1946 to 2007 in state-based armed conflicts—fighting between two armed groups, at least one of which is a

An UN Explosive Ordnance Disposal Unit uncovers an anti-tank mine in Syria.

A young woman receives occupational therapy after she lost her legs—and her 6-month old baby—in a landmine explosion in the Democratic Republic of the Congo.

government. Deaths have gradually decreased each decade, with the lowest numbers in current times: from 2002 to 2007, there were 100,846 casualties from state-based armed conflicts. In the same period, there were 19,788 deaths in non-state-based armed conflicts—fighting between two armed groups, neither of which is a government. Civilian casualties make up a startling 90 percent of deaths in conflict: for every soldier lost in war, nine civilians die.

On top of casualties, many millions more have been seriously injured, lost their means of making a living, or been forced to leave their homes and become *refugees*. Hundreds of thousands of children have become orphans as a direct result of war. Yet the struggle to survive is not over when a war ends. Thousands of people die from starvation or disease in war-torn countries that are unable to provide food, clean drinking water, or basic healthcare.

Since the end of World War II in 1945 till 2001, there have been 248 conflicts in 153 locations around the world. The US has been involved in 201 of those 248 overseas military conflicts, and it has launched operations in Afghanistan and Iraq since.

Additional Damage from Weapons

In many cases, the availability of arms has prolonged conflicts and hindered attempts at building peace. Communities emerging from war face major problems of crime, poverty, hunger, and disease. In addition, their industries, which provide jobs and income, as well as their basic *infrastructure*—including road and rail systems, hospitals, and power supplies—are frequently devastated by the violence.

Ironically, while there may be a scarcity of many basic necessities, arms are often found in abundance. With policing systems frequently not present, criminals, armed groups, and even desperate civilians often seek to use arms to obtain food

6

Efforts against the Arms Trade

Many people feel that the arms trade as it works today is wrong and produces undesirable, dangerous, and tragic effects. Work to counter the consequences of the arms trade occurs in many different ways, from the largest international conferences to the smallest mine-clearing projects.

Around the world, many charitable groups and agencies are trying to reduce the impact of arms and conflict on regions of the world. Dozens of organizations *lobby* governments and the UN for changes in the ways weapons are bought, sold, and used globally. Many other groups are concerned with the direct effects of arms use, treating war victims, rebuilding schools and hospitals, and helping refugees from conflicts settle in new places or return to their homes.

This statue of a knotted gun stands outside the United Nations headquarters in New York as a symbol of the organization's commitment to peace.

Arms Embargoes

Regulations on selling arms vary from country to country. Many nations have their own policies and refuse to sell certain types of arms or any at all to countries that are intent on war or use weapons against their own people. Sometimes countries group together, often through the UN, to impose an arms embargo—a ban on the sale of arms to a country. The UN arms embargo on South Africa, for example, started in 1977 and lasted until 1994. During that time, however, some arms supplies still managed to reach the country. Embargoes are rarely airtight, as seen with arms reaching embargoed countries including Sierra Leone, Libya, and Iraq.

Currently, the UN has mandatory arms embargoes on 13 countries and 3 groups: the countries with embargoes include Iran, Libya, North Korea, Somalia, and Sudan, and the 3 groups

Disarming People in Albania

Vast amounts of arms are in circulation in Albania—as many as one for every four people. A UN project is successfully removing some of these weapons from circulation by striking deals with villages to surrender arms in exchange for community projects such as better electricity supplies or new roads. Seran Llaha, a member of Tudge, a village which has joined the project, said, "I am very happy. All the village was involved. Giving in our guns is the first step for a safer, more peaceful future."

A member of a rebel group in Burundi surrenders his weapon and ammunition to a UN peacekeeping group, 2005.

The UN Security Council votes in 2014 to renew an arms embargo on Liberia.

are Al-Qaeda, the Taliban, and the Islamic State of Iraq and the Levant (ISIL).

End-User Certificates

In many international sales of arms, to get an export license, companies must now supply the government with an end-user certificate. This names who is buying the weapons and what they will use them for, certifying that the buyer is the final recipient of the arms and is not planning on transferring them to another party. While, in theory, this seems like a good idea, in practice, it does nothing to prevent an importer from promising to use arms for one purpose and then using them for another. For example, Hawk jet aircraft were sold by the UK to Indonesia with the intention of being used to patrol the country's borders. Instead, they were used in the summer of 2003 in attacks on Indonesia's own people in the Aceh province of the country.

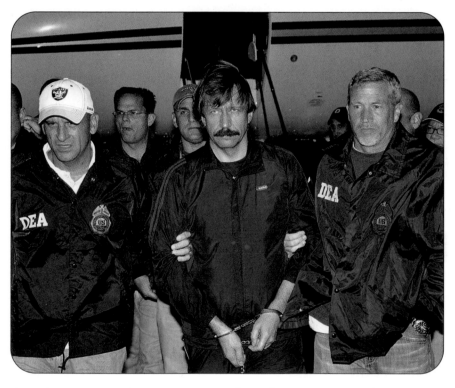

American Drug Enforcement Agency (DEA) agents escort Viktor Bout to the United States after his arrest in Thailand. Bout, a notorious Russian arms trader, sold weapons to a number of regimes and rebels in Africa and Asia. In 2011 he was convicted in a US court of selling anti-aircraft missiles and other weapons to the FARC, a rebel group in Colombia that the US government considers to be a terrorist organization. He was sentenced to 25 years in prison.

Grace Akallo, a former child soldier who participated in the conflict in Uganda, takes part in a UN Security Council debate on children and armed conflict, 2009.

License Loopholes

Some arms companies have tried to bypass restrictions on arms sales by disguising the true contents of the trade. In 1996, an export license was granted to a British company called Procurement Services International Ltd. for the sale of six water cannons to Indonesia, a license that also included "associated equipment." UK parliamentary questioning eventually revealed that the "associated equipment" included over 300 armored personnel carriers made by the British company,

Glover Webb. Despite this, the export license was not withdrawn by the government.

International Arms-Control Agreements

A number of international agreements that limit the sale and use of different weapons exist. The Nuclear *Nonproliferation* Treaty of 1970 aimed to prevent the proliferation, or spread, of nuclear weapons and technology, promote cooperation in peaceful uses of nuclear energy, and move toward nuclear and general disarmament. A total of 191 countries signed the treaty, more than any other arms-control agreement, perhaps because of the enormous potential harm involved in nuclear weapons.

The Biological Weapons Convention of 1975 and Chemical

 Transforming Guns into Hoes

Mozambique's civil war ended in 1992, but the large numbers of arms remaining in the country made rebuilding the nation extremely difficult. In 1995, the Mozambican Christian Council launched a campaign to "Transform Guns into Hoes." It sought to persuade people to hand over weapons in exchange for farming equipment, bicycles, and sewing machines. Thousands of guns, grenades, and landmines were traded in while people received useful, peaceful tools in return.

The Hiroshima Peace Memorial is the remains of one of the few buildings left standing after an atomic bomb was dropped on this Japanese city in August 1945. The atomic bombing killed more than 140,000 people. To prevent such devastating attacks in the future, the Nuclear Nonproliferation Treaty went into effect in 1970. The treaty was meant to prevent the spread of nuclear weapons, to promote cooperation in the peaceful uses of nuclear energy and to further the goal of achieving nuclear disarmament, as well as complete disarmament.

Weapons Convention of 1997 called for the prohibition of the development, production, stockpiling, and use of biological and chemical weapons, respectively, as well as their destruction.

There were several agreements specifically between the US and Soviet Union because of their superpower status and sheer size of armaments. The Intermediate-Range Nuclear Forces Treaty of 1988 was an agreement to eliminate their intermediate-range and shorter-range missiles. The Strategic Arms Reduction Treaty I of 1992 and Treaty II of 1997 were commitments to the reduction and limitation of strategic offensive arms.

The Arms Trade Treaty of 2013 established common international standards for regulating international trade in conventional arms and seeks to prevent and eradicate *illicit* trade in conventional arms.

The Ottawa Treaty

One of the most famous international arms agreements of recent years came into force in 1999. After years of campaigning, an agreement outlawing antipersonnel landmines was forged at the Ottawa Convention. The Ottawa Treaty, also known as the Mine Ban Treaty, is an internationally-binding agreement that bans the use, production, stockpiling, and transfer of antipersonnel mines. It also places responsibility on countries to clear affected areas, assist victims, and destroy stockpiles. It was hailed as a major breakthrough in controlling arms and has resulted in ongoing reports of landmine clearance. There are 162 nations that have signed the treaty, but the United States is not one of them.

Effectiveness of International Agreements

International agreements have had some success. For example, with the breakup of the Soviet Union in the 1990s, many newly-independent republics, such as Belarus, Ukraine, Georgia, and Kazakhstan, had Soviet nuclear weapons based on their soil which they removed and decommissioned before signing the Nuclear Nonproliferation Treaty. Nations involved in past conflicts, such as Eritrea or Congo, were originally opposed to signing the treaty, but eventually did so in the early 2000s.

However, for international agreements to work fully, all nations must sign and enforce the terms in the agreement. The three countries that are the largest producers of landmines—the US, Russia, and China—have not signed the Ottawa Treaty, nor have a number of other nations involved in an arms race with rival neighbors, such as North and South Korea.

Some arms companies are working to find ways around the landmines treaty. They are developing or fitting antitank mines, which are not banned by the treaty, with highly sensitive trigger devices that can be set off by far less weight than a tank, such as a person or a small vehicle.

While most nations around the world have signed the Nuclear Nonproliferation Treaty, Israel, India, and Pakistan have not signed, and all

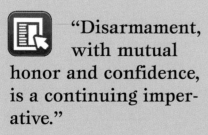

"Disarmament, with mutual honor and confidence, is a continuing imperative."

—former US President Dwight D. Eisenhower

three countries are believed to own or are working to develop nuclear weapons. In 2003, North Korea became the first nation to withdraw from the Nuclear Nonproliferation Treaty, and Iran decreased the level of access of international weapons inspectors to its nuclear facilities, leading to fears that both countries may be developing their own nuclear weapons. It was discovered that Iran failed to declare its uranium enrichment program—the foundation for nuclear arms capabilities—and defied the UN in continuing on with the program. In 2010, President Obama spoke on behalf of the US, Russia, and other nations, demanding that Iran face consequences for failing to adhere to the Nuclear Nonproliferation Treaty.

A government official sets fire to a pile of rifles collected during a gun amnesty in Abidjan, Côte d'Ivoire, in order to stop them from being used in future conflicts.

The Power of the People

Faced with the huge size and power of the arms trade, backed by many national governments, it is tempting to believe that ordinary people are powerless against the proliferation of weapons. This need not be the case. By banding together in groups to protest and campaign against aspects of the arms trade, ordinary people can make a difference. For example, the Ottawa Treaty banning landmines was partly the result of prolonged campaigns in many countries by civilian groups. One organization, the International Campaign to Ban Landmines, a *non-governmental organization* (NGO), received a Nobel Peace Prize in 1997 for its efforts in highlighting the damage landmines cause around the world.

Groups like the Campaign for Nuclear Disarmament (CND), Oxfam, Saferworld, and the Campaign against Arms Trade (CAAT) have highlighted and publicized arms-trade issues such as government subsidies for weapons makers. Human rights groups, including Amnesty International and Human Rights Watch, bring attention to atrocities committed by nations using arms. In the past, topics like these were not discussed openly in public, but today, they are debated in the media while pressure is placed on governments to change laws and regulations.

Future of the Arms Trade

It is highly unlikely that the arms trade will ever end. Arms will always be developed, bought, and sold while nations exist and believe there are threats to their security. Money will also be a constant motive for the distribution of weapons.

However, campaign groups believe it is possible to radically reduce the amount of arms dealt and increasingly restrict their use. Banning one type of weapon, reducing the sales of weapons to areas in conflict, or helping to disarm former soldiers in a region may only seem like small steps, yet they can make an enormous difference to the lives of many people.

 Text-Dependent Questions

1. Give one example of a treaty or agreement that was successful and one that was not completely successful.
2. Name two ways civilian groups have made a difference to help people against the arms trade.

 Research Project

Using the Internet or your school library, research the topic of the United Nations and the arms trade, and answer the following question: "Is the UN an effective authority against the arms trade?"

Some think that the UN is not effective because it cannot force countries to comply with international policies. If nations such as Iran refused to cooperate with restrictions on something as serious as nuclear weapons development, the UN has little power to stop them because it takes too long for so many countries to agree on a course of action, and the UN has limited ability to use force itself. Others say that the UN is an able authority against the arms trade because it brings international arms violations to the public eye. It can coordinate trade embargoes that impact illegal arms traders, and it can also bring together military forces from multiple countries. The UN has an important role as the entity that sets the necessary standards for what is and is not acceptable in the arms trade.

Write a two-page report, using data you have found in your research to support your conclusion, and present it to your class.

中国航天科技集团公司
China Aerospace Science and Technology Corporation

Global Arms Expenditures

Countries with the Highest Total Military Expenditures

Country	Military Expenditures
United States	$609.914 billion
People's Republic of China	$216.371 billion
Russian Federation	$84.462 billion
Saudi Arabia	$80.762 billion
France	$62.289 billion
United Kingdom of Great Britain	$60.482 billion
India	$49.968 billion
Germany	$46.455 billion
Japan	$45.776 billion
Republic of Korea (South Korea)	$36.677 billion
Brazil	$31.744 billion
Italy	$30.909 billion
Australia	$25.411 billion
United Arab Emirates	$22.755 billion

Turkey	$22.618 billion
Canada	$17.452 billion
Israel	$15.908 billion
Colombia	$13.054 billion
Spain	$12.732 billion
Algeria	$11.862 billion
Poland	$10.499 billion
Taiwan	$10.244 billion
Netherlands	$10.086 billion
Singapore	$9.841 billion
Oman	$9.623 billion
Iraq	$9.516 billion
Mexico	$8.660 billion
Pakistan	$8.537 billion
Indonesia	$7.020 billion
Angola	$6.842 billion
Norway	$6.773 billion
Sweden	$6.573 billion
Thailand	$5.730 billion
Venezuela	$5.576 billion
Greece	$5.318 billion
Switzerland	$5.229 billion
Belgium	$5.190 billion
Chile	$5.149 billion
Egypt	$4.961 billion
Malaysia	$4.919 billion

Source: SIPRI Database, Military Expenditure
by Country, in Current US$, 2014

The F-16 is one of the most widely sold fighter jets in the world. Countries including Israel and the United Arab Emirates have bought these aircraft from the United States.

Countries with Highest Military Expenditures as Percentage of Gross Domestic Product (GDP), 2014

Country	Percent of GDP Used on Military Expenditures
Oman	11.8 percent
Saudi Arabia	10.8 percent
South Sudan	8.2 percent
Libya	8.0 percent
United Arab Emirates	5.7 percent
Algeria	5.6 percent
Israel	5.2 percent
Republic of Congo	5.0 percent
Azerbaijan	4.8 percent
Lebanon	4.6 percent
Russian Federation	4.5 percent
Iraq	4.3 percent
Bahrain	4.2 percent
Namibia	4.2 percent
Armenia	4.0 percent
Guinea	3.8 percent
Myanmar	3.7 percent
Morocco	3.7 percent
Jordan	3.5 percent
United States	3.5 percent
Colombia	3.5 percent
Pakistan	3.4 percent

Kyrgyz Republic	3.4 percent
Singapore	3.2 percent
Brunei Darussalam	3.1 percent
Ukraine	3.1 percent
Mauritania	2.9 percent
Ecuador	2.7 percent
Lithuania	2.7 percent
Republic of Korea (South Korea)	2.6 percent
Zimbabwe	2.6 percent
India	2.4 percent
Georgia	2.3 percent
Sri Lanka	2.3 percent
Vietnam	2.3 percent
Greece	2.3 percent
France	2.2 percent
Turkey	2.2 percent
Lesotho	2.2 percent
Serbia	2.2 percent
China	2.1 percent

Source: The World Bank,
Military Expenditure (% of GDP)

North Korea spends a large percentage of its national budget on weapons and the armed forces. It uses state occasions to parade its military strength.

Countries with Largest Total Military Personnel, 2015

Country	Total Military Personnel
People's Republic of China	2,945,000
India	2,647,150
United States	1,520,100
Dem. Rep. of Korea (North Korea)	1,379,000
Russian Federation	1,364,000
Pakistan	946,000
Egypt	835,500
Brazil	713,480
Indonesia	676,500
Republic of Korea (South Korea)	659,500
Turkey	612,800
Islamic Republic of Iran.	563,000
Vietnam	522,000
Myanmar	513,250
Colombia	440,224
Thailand	474,550
Italy	367,550
Afghanistan	340,350
Mexico	329,750
France	332,250
Algeria	317,200
Sudan	264,300
Japan	260,086
Saudi Arabia	249,000
Morocco	245,800

Sri Lanka	223,100
Bangladesh	220,950
Spain	215,700
Eritrea	201,750
Peru	192,000

Source: The World Bank,
Armed Forces Personnel, Total

Largest Arms Importers, 2015

Country	Import Value
Saudi Arabia	$3.161 billion
India	$3.078 billion
Australia	$1.574 billion
Egypt	$1.475 billion
United Arab Emirates	$1.289 billion
Iraq	$1.215 billion
China	$1.214 billion
Vietnam	$870 million
Greece	$762 million
Pakistan	$735 million
Indonesia	$683 million
Taiwan (ROC)	$681 million
Qatar	$655 million
Bangladesh	$653 million
Algeria	$636 million

Israel	$617 million
Italy	$596 million
United States	$565 million
Mexico	$500 million
Turkey	$448 million
Kazakhstan	$419 million
Canada	$395 million
United Kingdom	$382 million
Kuwait	$366 million
Myanmar	$320 million
Japan	$310 million
Brazil	$289 million
Azerbaijan	$285 million
South Korea	$245 million
Finland	$228 million
Colombia	$215 million
Jordan	$198 million
Malaysia	$190 million
Nigeria	$188 million
Thailand	$185 million
Peru	$169 million
Belarus	$164 million
Venezuela	$162 million
Philippines	$158 million
Spain	$153 million
Oman	$148 million

Source: SIPRI Database,
TIV of Arms Exports from All, 2014-2015

Largest Arms Exporters, 2015

Country	Export Value
United States	$10,484 billion
Russian Federation	$5,483 billion
Germany	$2,049 billion
France	$2,013 billion
People's Republic of China	$1,966 billion
Spain	$1,279 billion
United Kingdom	$1,214 billion
Israel	$710 million
Italy	$570 million
Netherlands	$444 million
Switzerland	$369 million
Ukraine	$323 million
Canada	$312 million
Turkey	$291 million
Sweden	$186 million
Norway	$155 million
Czech Republic	$120 million
Australia	$113 million
South Korea	$105 million
United Arab Emirates	$63 million
Singapore	$48 million
Brazil	$41 million
South Africa	$39 million
Uzbekistan	$34 million
India	$33 million

Egypt	$22 million
Serbia	$19 million
Jordan	$18 million
Finland	$16 million
Denmark	$15 million
Austria	$14 million
Belarus	$14 million
Poland	$14 million
New Zealand	$7 million
Portugal	$7 million
Malta	$5 million
Indonesia	$4 million
Taiwan (ROC)	$4 million

Source: SIPRI Database,
TIV of Arms Exports to All, 2014-2015

Organizations to Contact

Campaign against Arms Trade

Unit 4, 5-7 Wells Terrace

London UK

N4 3JU

https://www.caat.org.uk/

Child Soldiers International

9 Marshalsea Road

London UK

SE1 1EP

http://www.child-soldiers.org/

International Campaign to Ban Landmines

ICBL-CMC

Maison de la Paix

2, Chemin Eugène-Rigot

CH-1202 Geneva

Switzerland

http://www.icbl.org/en-gb/home.aspx

Amnesty International

Calle Luz Saviñon 519

Colonia del Valle
Benito Juarez 03100
Ciudad de Mexico
https://www.amnesty.org/en/

Federation of American Scientists
Arms Sales Monitoring Project
1725 DeSales Street NW, Suite 600
Washington, DC 20036
http://fas.org/

Arms Control Association
1313 L Street, NW, Suite 130
Washington, DC 20005
http://www.armscontrol.org/

Human Rights Watch
350 Fifth Avenue, 34th Floor
New York, NY 10118-3299
https://www.hrw.org/

Series Glossary

apartheid—literally meaning "apartness," the political policies of the South African government from 1948 until the early 1990s designed to keep peoples segregated based on their color.

BCE and CE—alternatives to the traditional Western designation of calendar eras, which used the birth of Jesus as a dividing line. BCE stands for "Before the Common Era," and is equivalent to BC ("Before Christ"). Dates labeled CE, or "Common Era," are equivalent to *Anno Domini* (AD, or "the Year of Our Lord").

colony—a country or region ruled by another country.

democracy—a country in which the people can vote to choose those who govern them.

detention center—a place where people claiming asylum and refugee status are held while their case is investigated.

ethnic cleansing—an attempt to rid a country or region of a particular ethnic group. The term was first used to describe the attempt by Serb nationalists to rid Bosnia of Muslims.

house arrest—to be detained in your own home, rather than in prison, under the constant watch of police or other government forces, such as the army.

reformist—a person who wants to improve a country or an institution, such as the police force, by ridding it of abuses or faults.

republic—a country without a king or queen, such as the US.

United Nations—an international organization set up after the end of World War II to promote peace and co-operation throughout the world. Its predecessor was the League of Nations.

UN Security Council—the permanent committee of the United Nations that oversees its peacekeeping operations around the world.

World Bank—an international financial organization, connected to the United Nations. It is the largest source of financial aid to developing countries.

World War I—A war fought in Europe from 1914 to 1918, in which an alliance of nations that included Great Britain, France, Russia, Italy, and the United States defeated the alliance of Germany, Austria-Hungary, the Ottoman Empire, and Bulgaria.

World War II—A war fought in Europe, Africa, and Asia from 1939 to 1945, in which the Allied Powers (the United States, Great Britain, France, the Soviet Union, and China) worked together to defeat the Axis Powers (Germany, Italy, and Japan).

Further Reading

Carlson, Jennifer. *Citizen-Protectors: The Everyday Politics of Guns in an Age of Decline.* New York: Oxford University Press, 2015.

Cook, Philip J. *The Gun Debate: What Everyone Needs to Know.* New York: Oxford University Press, 2014.

Erickson, Jennifer. *Dangerous Trade: Arms Exports, Human Rights, and International Reputation.* New York: Columbia University Press, 2015.

Schroeder, Matthew. *The Small Arms Trade: A Beginner's Guide.* London: Oneworld Publications, 2012.

Stohl, Rachel, and Suzette Grillot. *The International Arms Trade.* Cambridge: Polity Books, 2013.

Internet Resources

www.caat.org.uk/

Campaign Against Arms Trade (CAAT) is a UK-based organization working to end the international arms trade by working to stop the export of arms that cause conflict; end all government political and financial support for arms exports; and promote progressive demilitarization within arms-producing countries. The website provides general to specific information on the arms trade, resources, and ways to get involved in the issue.

www.sipri.org/

The Stockholm International Peace Research Institute is an independent international institute dedicated to research into conflict, armaments, arms control, and disarmament. It provides data, analysis and recommendations to policymakers, researchers, media, and the interested public.

www.icbl.org/en-gb/home.aspx

International Campaign to Ban Landmines is a global network of non-governmental organizations, active in around 100 countries, that works for a world free of antipersonnel landmines, where landmine survivors can lead fulfilling lives. It includes details of the Ottawa Treaty and reports on landmine contamination and progress in clearing landmines.

http://www.saferworld.org.uk

Saferworld is an independent international organization working to prevent violent conflict and build safer
lives. It provides news, calls to action, and opinion
articles on world safety issues, including the arms
trade.

http://www.iaea.org

The International Atomic Energy Agency works with
its Member States and multiple partners worldwide to
promote the safe, secure, and peaceful use of nuclear
technologies. The website contains many reports and
resources on nuclear weapons and how the IAEA and
other organizations try to inspect sites and increase
safety.

Index

Numbers in **bold italics** refer to captions.

About the Author

Dan Marcovitz studied history at Western Kentucky University. He works as a freelance writer and editor. This is his first book for young people.

Picture Credits: Everett Historical: 42; Library of Congress: 11; National Museum of the US Air Force: 46; used under license from Shutterstock, Inc.: 1, 2, 9, 22, 39, 50, 53, 54, 82, 88; Sarine Arslanian / Shutterstock.com: 6; Astrelok / Shutterstock.com: 94; Volodymyr Borodin / Shutterstock.com: 25; ChameleonsEye / Shutterstock.com: 34; Dmitry Chulov / Shutterstock.com: 59; Istvan Csak / Shutterstock.com: 66; Thomas D. Dittmer / Shutterstock.com: 91; Sadik Gulec / Shutterstock.com: 56; Anton Gvozdikov / Shutterstock.com: 26; Jointstar / Shutterstock.com: 21; Vladimir Melnik / Shutterstock.com: 32; Punghi / Shutterstock.com: 15; Jeremy Richards / Shutterstock.com: 60; Sementer / Shutterstock.com: 105; Jordan Tan / Shutterstock.com: 37; Dietmar Temps / Shutterstock.com: 24; Tinxi / Shutterstock.com: 18; Thor Jorgen Udvang / Shutterstock.com: 40; United Nations photo: 12, 27, 28, 30, 31, 45, 61, 62, 69, 72, 75, 77, 78, 80, 85; US Drug Enforcement Administration: 79; US Air Force: 16.